EMILIA TRIES THE CELLO

Written by: Katarina Majcen Pliego
Illustrated by: Jeannine Corcoran

Copyright © by Katarina Majcen Pliego
All rights reserved.

Thank you for buying an authorized edition of this book and for complying with copyright laws by not reproducing, scanning, or distributing any part of it in any form without permission.

ISBN: 979-8-35094-987-2

Printed in the Unites States of America.
Second edition: February 2024

To my Emilia,
the smartest, funniest,
and not-very-interested-in-music girl

Emilia was excited to put on her best dress,

and go with her family to a fancy event.

She's attending a concert, and is going to see

a symphony orchestra perform Giuseppe Verdi.

With a ticket in one hand, and toy in the other,

she finds her seat with her father and mother.

She listens to the strings, the brass, and the winds,

then she asks, "What is that big, brown thing?"

Her mom, a musician, explains it's a cello,

a string instrument that sounds real low and mellow.

Emilia, completely entranced,

immediately wants to get up and dance!

The very next morning she goes to her school

and picks up the cello to play a tune.

Endpin, four strings, and a bow,

there is just so much she must know!

With lots of hard work, slow practice, and patience, she progresses from bowing open strings to using all four fingers.

She can play on her own or she can play with her friends,

from classical to pop, the fun really never ends!

In addition to playing, she must also sing,

read notation in several clefs and keys.

Let's not forget about all those Italian terms

that Emilia now needs to learn.

The instrument can be different,

but music theory stays the same,

for all other instruments

she may want to play.

Tuba, bassoon, and horn,

Emilia is a little forlorn.

So many instruments, and it takes so much time,

just to learn "Twinkle Twinkle Little Star."

She's sharing her knowledge with her little sister,

telling her about practicing and playing *a vista*.

They're listening to famous composers, and cellists too,

enjoying everything the instruments and music can do.

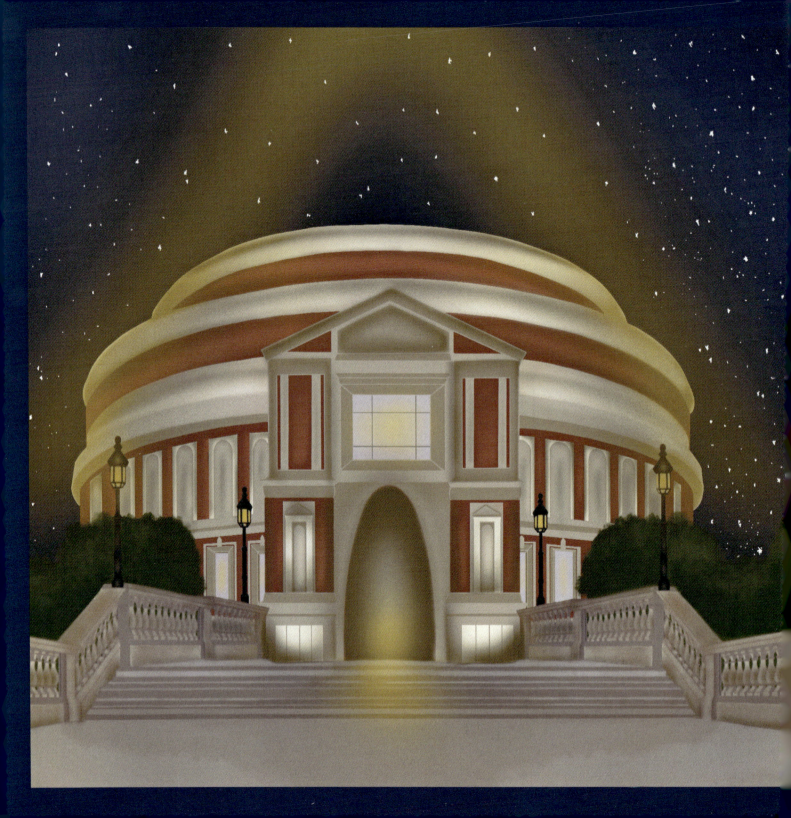

Glossary:

- *A vista* – playing music "at first sight" (no rehearsing)
- Clef – musical symbol used to indicate which notes are represented by the lines and spaces on the musical stave (five lines on which we place the notes). Most common clefs are treble, alto, and bass.
- Giuseppe Verdi – famous Italian Romantic composer in the nineteenth century
- Luthier – a person who makes string instruments
- Rosin – solid form of resin obtained from pines and other conifers
- Key – group of pitches, major or minor scale, around which a piece of music revolves
- Italian terms – Italian terms are commonly used to indicate tempo (speed), dynamic level, feel/emotion, repetitions, and more, throughout a piece written in Western classical tradition
- Music theory – study of concepts and compositional methods involved in the creation and understanding of music
- Notation – a system used to visually represent music. A series of symbols and markings that inform the musician how a piece of music should be performed.
- Chamber ensemble – a small group of musicians like a string quartet (two violins, viola, cello), piano trio (violin, cello, piano), clarinet trio (clarinet, piano, cello)

Cello facts:

- Cello (or violoncello) belongs to the string family (same as violin, viola, double bass, guitar, and harp).
- Cello has the same register as the human voice, making it very pleasant to listen to.
- The first cello was made in the early sixteenth century. It did not have an endpin, and the strings were made from sheep guts.
- The oldest existing cello is known as The King, and was built by a famous Italian luthier, Andrea Amati, between 1538 and 1560. It is on display at the National Museum in Vermillion, South Dakota.
- The instrument is made of different kinds of wood, usually with a spruce top and maple for the back and sides.
- The bow is made of Pernambuco wood and horsehair. It needs to have rosin put on the hair to make it sticky and playable.
- Cello is used in variety of ensembles, including the symphony orchestra, string orchestra, and different kinds of chamber ensembles.
- Cellos come in different sizes. From smallest to largest we have: an eighth, a quarter, a half, a three quarter, and a whole cello. The size depends on how tall the cellist is. Professionals play whole sized cellos, while the smaller sizes accommodate children.

*Scan me to access even more cello facts and resources.

Resources for parents:

- If your child is interested in a specific instrument, find a private instrumental teacher. Many can be found and contacted through local music schools and academies. Middle school and high school orchestra directors will usually also have a list of private teachers.
- If your child is unsure of which instrument to play, take them to an instrument petting zoo. These are mostly organized by local symphony orchestras. Your child will have an opportunity to hear, touch, and try all symphonic instruments there.
- String instruments can be taught as early as five years of age, when following the "traditional" method of teaching (learning how to read notes and rhythms right away).
- String instruments can be taught as early as three years of age, if following the Suzuki method (not reading the music but playing by ear). If choosing this method, please find a certified Suzuki teacher.
- Rent the instrument (many music shops will have a rent-to-own program).
- Speak to several private teachers and set up trial lessons. Many teachers will offer a trial lesson for free or at a reduced rate. You are not required to commit to weekly lessons immediately after the trial lesson. It is important to introduce your child to several teachers and their teaching style, and decide on one that your child is most comfortable with.
- Set up weekly instrumental lessons. Consistency is key.
- Set aside time for daily practice. The parent does not need to be present during instrumental lesson and practice time, but this is dependent on each child's personality.
- Encourage your child to listen to music!

Listening resources:

Johann Sebastian Bach (1685-1750): *Suite for Solo Cello no. 1 in G Major*

Ludwig van Beethoven (1770-1827): *Sonata for Cello and Piano no. 3 in A Major*

Johannes Brahms (1833-1897): *Sonata in E minor, Sonata in F major, Concerto for Violin and Cello in A Minor*

Antonin Dvořák (1841-1904): *Cello Concerto in B Minor*

Sir Edward Elgar (1857-1934): *Cello Concerto in E minor*

Gabriel Fauré (1845-1924): *Apres un Reve, Elegie, Papillon*

Sofia Gubaidulina (*1931): *Canticle of the Sun, Mirage: The Dancing Sun*

Joseph Haydn (1732-1809): *Cello Concerto in C Major, Cello Concerto in D Major*

David Popper (1843-1913): *Hungarian Rhapsody, Elfentanz*

Camille Saint-Saëns (1835-1921): *The Swan, Allegro Appassionato*

Giovanni Sollima (*1962): *Lamentatio, Violoncelles Vibrez!*

*Scan me to access the playlist with all the listening resources.